W9-AJQ-160

Woodstock, Vermont 05091

ADOBE

ORLANDO ROMERO AND DAVID LARKIN

BUILDING AND LIVING WITH EARTH

PHOTOGRAPHY BY MICHAEL FREEMAN

A DAVID LARKIN BOOK

HOUGHTON MIFFLIN COMPANY

BOSTON   NEW YORK

1994

TEXT COPYRIGHT © 1994 BY ORLANDO ROMERO

COMPILATION COPYRIGHT © 1994 BY DAVID LARKIN

ALL RIGHTS RESERVED

FOR INFORMATION ABOUT PERMISSION TO REPRODUCE
SELECTIONS FROM THIS BOOK, WRITE TO PERMISSIONS,
HOUGHTON MIFFLIN COMPANY, 215 PARK AVENUE SOUTH,
NEW YORK, NEW YORK 10003.

LIBRARY OF CONGRESS CATALOGING-IN-PUBLICATION DATA

ROMERO, ORLANDO, DATE.
ADOBE / BUILDING AND LIVING WITH EARTH / ORLANDO ROMERO AND DAVID
LARKIN : PHOTOGRAPHY BY MICHAEL FREEMAN.
P. CM.
"A DAVID LARKIN BOOK."
INCLUDES BIBLIOGRAPHICAL REFERENCES.
ISBN 0-395-56693-2
1. BUILDING, ADOBE. I. LARKIN, DAVID. II. TITLE.
NA4145.A35R65 1994
721'.04422 — DC20   94-11692
                                                                          CIP

PRINTED IN ITALY BY SFERA/GARZANTI, MILAN

SFE 10 9 8 7 6 5 4 3 2 1

CONTENTS

Introduction

AT FIRST GLANCE, adobe appears to the eye and the mind as a contradiction. How is it possible to build, out of mud, a simple one-room shelter, let alone a magnificent residence, mosque, or monastery? How is it possible that this fragile composition of soil, straw, and labor has lasted centuries, nurturing and sustaining countless cultures, even including early human habitation in North America? What dreams, energies, fortunes, fantasies, and spiritual yearnings have been fulfilled or have died in creating with mud? Adobe, mud though it is, is built to last. It will continue to survive as long as men and women understand their connection with their most important inheritance, the earth itself. We build shelter with that which is most available to us. And it is not surprising that an estimated one third of the world's population lives in earthen structures. Unlike many forms of architecture, adobe does not intrude on the horizon of human history. While building with adobe is inherently an enormous act of creativity, it is a benign act that is most often in total harmony with nature. An adobe structure, properly built, is in that earthen comfort zone that tempers the harshest of climates: it is efficient shelter in the searing desert heat of Arizona or Saudi Arabia, the windy reaches of East Anglia, or the snowy mountain regions of Asia.

Building with adobe begs participation. In building a home, for example, each member of the family plays a vital role. From the simplest act of mixing the mud for the adobe bricks or mixing the adobe mortar that cements each course, to the final plaster that will give adobe its sculptural beauty, the voices of young children blend in harmony with the movement of hands of all ages. The sense of creating shelter out of mud and earth is as primal as what must have been the first potter's amazement in creating an earthen vase; as the clay is manipulated, the potter gives it life and shape, resulting in a natural beauty that no straight line can offer. That is why adobe is so pleasing. It is the shape of the heart, the mystical connection that unifies man with nature. It has little to do with real estate; it offers a spiritual exchange that challenges man to give the earth life so that in return it can provide a nourishing protective womb that is as real and fragile as our lives.

A Personal Note by Orlando Romero.

For the individual, adobe is something from a past that reminds us that we must pay careful attention to the context of our lives, as we must to earthen structures. An adobe building, from foundation to roof, is a metaphor for attending to our lives and those protected by its walls. Left unchecked, a trickle of water from a neglected roof can bring down an entire wall. With a bit of attention and love, like our families, adobe structures have lasted generations, in fact centuries.

One must have lived in a properly built adobe structure in order to explain its mysteries, the sense of security one feels in it. The walls cannot burn, their thickness fights off the noisy world. Just as the massive masonry naturally adjusts to exterior temperatures, that very balance brings a great sense of well-being to the interior spaces and their inhabitants.

Some buildings made of earth, whether adobe or rammed earth, have been called symphonies in mud. I can think of no other material that so aptly fits such a description. Every movement in a symphony is created for the delight and pleasure of the listener. Great symphonies reveal birth, struggle, life; the moments of climax and intensity are balanced by interludes which reveal themselves as quiet insight available only to those who really listen. Adobe, then, is at times a peaceful interlude not understood by all but available to all who truly listen to the gentle murmur of our earth. Adobe in all its forms is the earth, our earth.

My grandfather used to say that the earth was full of sound. He didn't mean cars. He meant crickets, frogs and the echo of stars colliding in the intensity of the crowded Milky Way. How fitting, how intelligent for man to build out of that sound, that music. Adobe repels the discordant and amplifies the balanced sounds and music of life, death and rebirth.

Grandmother died in the adobe room my wife and I have shared as lovers for twenty-six years. This old adobe house has seen my children grow to adulthood. This house is not a shelter only, but a home for my ancient ancestors that came to this land in 1598. Some intermarried with the local Pueblo Indians and our history rebounds from wall to wall. All is contained within these earthen walls, a potent kind of magic that starts with the laying of hands on one adobe brick at a time until the protective shell is complete.

While the poet may struggle to describe adobe, the adobe practitioner does not. He and She know. They know that every brick and plaster stroke is power, not only the power of self-reliance but also the power of self-realization. With every new adobe course or summer remudding, they are reborn. Therein lies the real secret of working and living with adobe. I hope the following pages will not just enlighten you but make you want to join the family of adobe.

If nothing else, take a journey into adobe that begins by merely turning the page.

The African Connection

A strong architectural influence connects historic North and West Africa with the New World. The Moorish Islamic empire spread up into Spain and originated many styles and techniques of construction that later moved over the Atlantic with the conquistadors. The Moors had also pressed down into the rump of West Africa bearing similar influences. Today, we see their imprint on these vernacular buildings.

right
According to tradition, the Mosque of Nando was built in the twelfth century in a single night. It is the only adobe structure in a village of stone houses.

Tiny windows pierce the facade of a house in Mali. The small openings help prevent the entry of dust, harsh heat, and glaring sunlight.

The Great Mosque of Djenné, in Mali, West Africa, was rebuilt in 1907. Djenné occupies a peninsula surrounded by a river. The mosque's massive terrace prevents even the highest floodwaters from destroying the base of the monument.

The east facade of the Mosque of Djenné faces Mecca. In the foreground are the walls of a communal grave, resting place of important leaders, which was part of the large adobe mosque that stood on this site from the thirteenth to the twentieth century.

In the American Southwest, women are respected for their skills as *enjaradoras* (plasterers). In this photograph by Edward S. Curtis, Laguna Pueblo women remud an adobe home in 1925.

Replastering a house in Djenné with a fresh coat of mud.
Traditionally, trowels are never used; the work is done by
hand.

The New World

INDIANS IN MEXICO had long employed the adobe brick in building, but it was the Spaniards who would spread its use in the Southwest. In Mexico, for example, adobe comprised the structure of some of the great pyramids, which were then veneered with stone. Though we know that settled Pueblo Indians of the Southwest had contact with Mesoamerica, why did it take the Spanish to introduce to this area adobe bricks made in a form? Possibly the Pueblos preferred the traditional puddling method. Yet the introduction of the form-made brick, dried in the sun, revolutionized construction and resulted in a pleasing mixture of Spanish and Pueblo styles that is still copied.

Along with the form-made brick, the Spanish introduced the so-called kiva fireplace (corner fireplace) and the *horno*, in which bread and other foods are cooked today. While there is little doubt that the Spanish introduced the wonderful beehive outdoor ovens, similar ovens can be found in the Sichuan province of China.

Adobe is not merely something exotic found halfway around the world, nor is it confined, in the United States, to the romance of the Southwest. How many Americans know that the house of Paul Revere, perhaps the oldest in Boston (circa 1680), is made of unfired bricks laid between posts? Two hundred years later, adobe construction methods were still in use in New York and Washington, D.C.

In Geneva, New York, a number of adobe houses remain as testimony to this material's endurance. The preservationist Richard Pieper has documented that "forty mud brick structures . . . dotted a nine county area in New York that spanned half the State." Of fifteen mud brick residences constructed in mid-nineteenth-century New York, eleven are standing today. Few of these buildings seem to have been affected by the rigorous climate of the Northeast.

Despite the usefulness, endurance, and aesthetic appeal of adobe, a prejudice against mud buildings has long continued, perhaps due to misinformation about their durability and a dismissive attitude toward material that is so "common." When explored with an open mind, adobe presents uncommon potential. In 1842 Henry Ellsworth, the first U.S. commissioner of patents, built an experimental structure of unfired adobe bricks in Washington, D.C. Three years later, when he left the patent office and became an agent for federal lands, he proposed that adobe be used in the new settlements on the prairies.

According to Richard Pieper, Ellsworth and other pioneers had been guided by "the chain of translations and adaptations of publications on earthen architecture that had reached the United States in the nineteenth century." French publications on *pisé* (rammed-earth building) in 1791 documented experiments with adobe. This trend combined good timing and good sense. A young nation stretching westward needed adaptable housing, and the low cost of producing adobe bricks pointed toward self-reliance and independence. Adobe houses (such as the Lawrence Welk home in South Dakota) can still be seen on the midwestern prairies, where early pioneers built dwellings of earthen sod or sun-fired adobe bricks.

In the Spanish Southwest, from the Rio Grande to the beaches of California, adobe had long been the dominant and preferred building material. In Santa Fe, New Mexico, the Palace of the Governors (circa 1608) stands as testimony to adobe.

Few historic American buildings have withstood the conflicts and upheavals endured by the Palace of the Governors. In 1680 a group of Native Americans carried out the first and most successful revolt against the Spanish colonists, who fled toward El Paso. In 1693, the Spaniards reconquered Santa Fe and regained the palace. The Mexican government took possession of the area in 1821; the palace was briefly seized by rebels in 1837; after the struggles of the Mexican War, the U.S. government took charge, although the Confederate flag flew briefly over this historic adobe structure during the Confederates' short-lived attempt to reach the gold fields of California.

In 1909 the Palace of the Governors became a museum. Today indigenous peoples quietly sell their wares at its door, while inside, exhibits document the influence of Hispanic, French, Native American, and other peoples who have added to the richness and diversity of Santa Fe's history. Massive adobe walls frame this very American confluence of cultures.

Outdoor adobe cooking ovens are commonplace in both Hispanic village and Pueblo plaza. Though the majority of these adobe walls conceal their vigas (the supporting round beams that span a roof), five vigas protrude from a weathered adobe wall. The Spaniards introduced saws and other woodworking implements that made it easier to fashion vigas of the precise length needed, eliminating the protruding vigas that can succumb to the harsh climate of northern New Mexico. Yet traditional ways persist despite Old World influences.

Earthen buildings, which appear to be fragile, can be found in the most inhospitable regions. From the searing heat of desert valleys to the dizzying altitude of snow-covered mountains, well-maintained adobe houses may outlast the builder's lifetime and continue to provide shelter for generations.

Yet each season of the year poses particular problems for adobe dwellings. March's buffeting winds may lightly scar raw adobe. July's rains pose the greatest problem, especially if a building's roof is in poor condition or if its stem walls aren't high enough off the ground to prevent basal erosion. Fall is usually kinder to adobe, but winter's rigors and repeated wetting and freezing of raw adobe walls can be devastating. Despite these adversities, adobe has lasted centuries in the most severe climates. Studies show that it can take decades to wear a few inches off an adobe wall, and this erosion can be easily remedied with an inexpensive plaster of the same earth.

Adobe masonry requires little exploitation of natural resources; when abandoned, an adobe structure returns to the elements that gave it birth. Living with a natural adobe home teaches a person to live with nature and to prepare for the arrival of each season. A heightened awareness of earth and the elements has given builders in adobe a knack for creating structures that maximize nature's benefits and deflect its assaults. Adobe builders generally plan doors, windows, and courtyards to face southern exposures, bathing their homes with light during the winter months.

Spanish settlement in the New World introduced Old World Moorish architectural traditions such as the enclosed patio and courtyard. The smaller *plazuela* (family courtyard) contained architectural elements based on Spanish preferences and the need for defense. Large enclosed courtyards such as these provided protection for settlers and their livestock. A successful, defensible courtyard required access to water. In essence, this courtyard was self-sufficient, and in times of peace courtyards like these saw much cultural interchange.

This historic adobe hacienda now stands as a monument to the priest Antonio José Martinez, a local hero to the Hispanic people of New Mexico, though he was in constant conflict with his French archbishop in the 1850s, Jean-Baptiste Lamy. Martinez was eventually suspended from his priestly duties, but his dynamism and intellect became a powerful force in Taos. He established a school there, published works printed on his own press, served as a delegate to the Mexican territorial legislature in Santa Fe, and fought a running war with his ecclesiastical superiors, defending the practices and privileges of the Penitentes.

This reconstructed room of frontier New Mexico exemplifies a Spanish Colonial dwelling. Small doors aided in defense and in protection from New Mexico's harsh climate. The door's frame serves as a hinge, pegged at bottom and top, to allow the door to swing in.

The room's sparse furnishings bespeak the hardships and survival skills of Spanish colonists: braided horsehair lariats, an adze, wool shears, a powder horn, a buffalo lance, buffalo hunters, a *petaquilla* (leather chest), dried corn and chile, and an Indian *metate* (grindstone). The frontier allowed few luxuries, and the settlers' life was more like that of their Pueblo neighbors than the life they left in Mexico.

The Weather

Earthen buildings, which appear to be fragile, can be found in the most inhospitable regions. From the searing heat of desert valleys to the dizzying altitude of snow-covered mountains, well-maintained adobe houses may outlast the builder's lifetime and continue to provide shelter for generations.

Yet each season of the year poses particular problems for adobe dwellings. March's buffeting winds may lightly scar raw adobe. July's rains pose the greatest problem, especially if a building's roof is in poor condition or if its stem walls aren't high enough off the ground to prevent basal erosion. Fall is usually kinder to adobe, but winter's rigors and repeated wetting and freezing of raw adobe walls can be devastating. Despite these adversities, adobe has lasted centuries in the most severe climates. Studies show that it can take decades to wear a few inches off an adobe wall, and this erosion can be easily remedied with an inexpensive plaster of the same earth.

Adobe masonry requires little exploitation of natural resources; when abandoned, an adobe structure returns to the elements that gave it birth. Living with a natural adobe home teaches a person to live with nature and to prepare for the arrival of each season. A heightened awareness of earth and the elements has given builders in adobe a knack for creating structures that maximize nature's benefits and deflect its assaults. Adobe builders generally plan doors, windows, and courtyards to face southern exposures, bathing their homes with light during the winter months.

The buttresses of San Francisco de Taos Church illustrate both the sculptural potential of adobe and some difficulties in maintaining it. Cracks in the surface's hard cement plaster may allow rain and melting snow to seep in, at times undetected, causing damage to the adobe underneath. One solution to this problem is stripping the building of its hard plaster, allowing the adobe to breathe and to dry naturally. This technique has been used with success on some historic buildings, but it requires remudding the building every few years—a formidable task when the adobe structure is large and the work force consists of local villagers and other volunteers.

Unprotected, the unattended wisps of memories of a bygone
era dissolve into the same earth that gave this structure
life. One can only imagine the human energy expended
to build this homestead, a reminder of mortality and
our connectedness to the earth. Unlike a ghost town of
dilapidated wooden buildings, adobe's deterioration is more
graceful, more natural.

It may take another half-century before these defiant walls
completely succumb to the weather. Or perhaps another
builder will reuse this earth and begin a new cycle of dreams,
learning to live with the weather and adobe.

Construction

ADOBE is the most plastic and forgiving of all building materials. As P. G. McHenry, Jr., author of *Adobe: Build It Yourself,* has stated, "Adobe is the ideal material for the beginner. It is a warm, kind material that is forgiving of mistakes, and amenable to change. If you don't like what you have wrought, it is a simple matter to take it down and try again."

Yet building with adobe is labor-intensive. The standard adobe brick weighs somewhere between twenty-five and thirty pounds—imagine the labor involved in carrying, lifting, and setting the two to six thousand adobe bricks needed to build a typical house. Today most adobe bricks are mass-produced and delivered to the building site. Yet some self-reliant individuals make their own bricks.

Anyone who has built an adobe home can tell you of aching muscles—and the joy of working with the materials. My grandfather, who constructed many an adobe building, believed it had to do with the smell of wet mud mixed as mortar and its pleasing texture. Working in adobe is akin to shaping pottery by the coil method—both the tactile pleasure and the satisfaction of seeing the walls build up, round by round.

Building with adobe is extremely physical; mixing the mud for mortar and securely placing every adobe demand dexterity, patience, perseverance, and disciplined creativity. The mason (often self-taught) must plan ahead and pay close attention to mundane details. Good, strong footings and stem walls are a must. If the structure is to have a flat roof, *canales* (rain spouts) must be built to direct rainwater away from walls.

Though many in the Southwest aspire to the "adobe look," no amount of plaster or curved walls forced out of rigid two-by-sixes can produce the feeling of adobe construction. That feeling begins with the use of earth as a shelter, the acknowledgment that this form of shelter is not the privilege of the rich, but is for all who have inherited the earth. Adobe homes have included magnificent residences, haciendas that are now part of the vogue, the fashion, of the privileged classes, but it is important to understand that adobe construction also frees and brings self-reliance and creativity to anyone who is willing to experience adobe construction.

Classic adobe yards like this one, built around 1950, were a common sight throughout New Mexico before large commercial yards made their appearance in the 1970s. By the number of the adobes already stacked, it is clear that this too was a commercial yard; the difference is that here all the labor was done by hand.

If a couple of sixteen-year-old boys were unemployed in the summer, it wasn't unusual to see an acre or two of family land converted into an adobe yard. Many a young Hispanic boy made enough money to buy his clothes for the school year by making adobes during the summer, and there were always plenty of eager customers. The work was back-breaking but the experience was worth gaining, especially when it became his turn to make adobes for his own home.

Adobe Making

Making adobe bricks by hand in the traditional way usually takes at least two persons. Once the adobe mud is mixed with straw, the brick forms must be thoroughly wetted so that the mud mixture will easily slide out. The adobe mold, or form, used here is for a specialized brick—thus its unusually small size. Note how the form is closed on one side; the usual form is open on both sides. The process, however, is typical of all handmade adobe bricks.

The mixing of the mud is critical. The earth and straw must be combined thoroughly, and the earth must be free of large stones and pebbles that might later cause the brick to crack. Traditionally, mounds or pits where mud is mixed with straw may be ten feet in diameter or larger.

Once the mud is ready, the mold is carefully filled and packed down so that the resulting brick does not have any cracks or air pockets.

Adobe molds may be of various sizes, depending on the use of the brick, and may have as many as six cavities. The larger the mold, the more difficult it is to lift once the mud has filled the cavities.

No matter what size the resulting bricks may be, the designer must ensure that handles are provided for lifting the mold once the cavities have been filled with mud. This small mold seems to be of ancient vintage, handmade and pegged together with very small nails.

The mold must be lifted precisely and evenly so the soft bricks separate cleanly from the mold.

Once the bricks are removed from the mold, they are left to dry in the sun. After a few days, if the weather is good, they are turned on their narrow sides so that sun and air continue to "bake" the brick.

In many Hispanic and Native American communities, the season for making adobe bricks was part of a ritual as important as sacred feast days. The month of July particularly was avoided, because moisture-laden clouds that rose over the Jemez Mountains could destroy two weeks' worth of brick-building in less than half an hour of torrential rains.

As the courses of adobe bricks go up, the string is adjusted to receive the next course. Note that in this case the string is attached to a framing buck, whereas the other side of the string may be anchored to a number of adobes that have been leveled horizontally.

Once the string is adjusted, the mason can repeat the process of firmly laying the adobe, one course at a time, until the wall reaches the appropriate height. If cement is used as mortar, then the *albañil* (mason) must trowel all joints clean to avoid mortar buildup. Adobe mortar is more forgiving and will easily chip off should the mason forget to trowel clean a joint or two.

Lintels may be made of pine, fir, or even cast cement but must be level to accept a window or door frame. Note the "gringo block" to the left of the rough frame below the lintel. This block allows anchoring of the frame to the adobe wall. The term perhaps originated when Anglo Americans started to build adobe homes and needed a method to anchor frames to adobe masonry.

The Picuris Story

In 1776, Fray Atanasio Dominguez, in his now-famous "Description of New Mexico," noted that he was taking inventory of a new structure at the pueblo of Picuris. The older mission church had been ordered torn down by governor Don Pedro Fermin de Medinveta, "because the pueblo is isolated and therefore indefensible against the continual incursions which the Comanche enemy is making. These raids are so daring that this father I have mentioned assured me that he escaped by a miracle in '69 for they sacked the convent and destroyed his meager supplies; yet he considered them well spent in exchange for his life and freedom from captivity."

What the Comanche couldn't do to this newer mission church, time and the elements did. When their Native American mission church collapsed, the Picuris Pueblo people rallied around the rebuilding of their church. Communally they work together much like their ancient ancestors in preserving their native religion as well as their Catholic faith.

The vigas (round beams) in the foreground are essential to the rebuilding process if the structure is to be historically accurate. Before they are placed on the walls, all bark must be carefully peeled off to avoid infestation and damage by parasites living in the bark. The longer the span a viga has to cover, the wider in diameter it must be. Vigas are critical in the construction phase because they help anchor adobe walls and will be load-bearing once they are attached to the walls.

Looking more like a pre-Columbian, Mesoamerican temple at this stage, this mission church will almost double its present height. The massive buttresses are not only historically correct but also keep the walls from leaning outward. Layered adobe courses in the wall and partially plastered buttresses direct the eye to a lone cross that is positioned where the altar will be. In this phase of building, the scene is reminiscent of the early Pecos or Jemez mission ruins.

Viewing the walls from an elevated position shows how adobe bricks must be "woven" or "tied" when building massive walls. At certain intervals adobe bricks may be laid in two rows that are fourteen inches across, then two rows that are ten inches across, with varied spaces in between, forming a woven pattern and giving the wall its constant thickness. Any pattern will work as long as it is consistent.

During later stages of construction, as mud plastering begins, the rectangular form of the adobe brick will be transformed into curving lines that defy a straight linear perspective. The plain adobe bricks will be covered by a mud plaster as richly textured as the landscape.

As the mission church continues to grow in height, the mighty buttresses at the rear of the church begin to take shape. Once the church is plastered, it will appear to rise directly from the earth, giving the structure a tremendous sense of solidity.

Where there is light, there is shadow, and the simplest beauty of adobe is the way the light plays on its textures and angles. It is absolutely necessary to build a strong footing so that the first few rows of adobes that make up the wall are well above ground level. The higher the footing, the less likely that basal erosion will undermine the adobe masonry. Coving caused by basal erosion can threaten an entire adobe structure.

Five adobe courses later, this pueblo's mission church continues to grow toward the sky. Additional adobe *padercitas* (small walls) enhance the mission's entrance, in contrast to the rounded buttresses.

The last remnants of the adobe walls leading into the mission church's courtyard await restoration. The priority is the mission itself, but this ancient wall, with its many layers of mud plaster and its whitewashed surface, will also be attended to.

Plastering

A natural, weathered adobe wall is all texture. One can compare it to a favorite nubby tweed jacket that has experienced the world upon one's back and tasted the elements of life. Here, new adobes, smooth and symmetrical, contrast beautifully with adobes that may be hundreds of years old. Though natural adobe walls require regular maintenance, the work becomes a kind of ritual that connects the owner to the cycle of the seasons. Once the weather is free of frost, many villages in New Mexico will restore their adobe buildings before July's rains appear.

True adobe restoration must take into account the original builder's whims and sensibilities. It is always a difficult decision, whether to follow this original intent or to explore current adobe styles. Here, the restorer has decided to expose the double row of lintels to continue the graceful curve of the wall as it meets the lintel post, which, more than likely, was the intention of the original builder.

Part of the joy of living in a northern New Mexico village is watching an *albañil* (adobe mason) working with natural, unstabilized adobe. Here, the *albañil* has prepared to restore a natural adobe wall by first wetting the original last course with water and adding a new layer of adobe mortar to bond the new adobes. His almost dancelike movements are as graceful as the corners left by the weathered wall.

right
The first rough coat of plaster, while still wet, must be scored with a rake or a special grooved trowel. The scoring allows the final smooth coat of plaster to adhere to the wall.

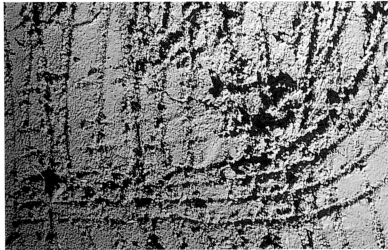

Native American and Hispanic women have a long and continuous involvement in adobe construction. From making the bricks to building the fireplaces to actual construction, their roles have been vital to the survival of adobe, and of their cultures as well.

In Fray Alonso de Benavides's "Memorial of 1630," he noted of Pueblo women that "among these nations it is the custom of the women to build the walls; the men spin and weave their *mantas,* and go to war and the chase; and if we [try to] oblige some men to build walls, he runs away from it, and the women laugh. And with this [work of women] there have been built more than fifty churches with roofs, [with] very beautiful carvings and fretwork, and the walls well painted."

Today, women of both cultures might also participate in building an adobe structure. They are always sought for their skills as *enjaradoras.* The saying in Hispanic culture is *El hombre las levanta, la mujer las enjara*—"The man builds the walls and the woman plasters them."

While the men supply a steady flow of mud mixed with straw, the women plaster the walls in unison. Although different women may plaster separate sections, their work results in a uniformly smooth, even surface (see left of door).

right

As soon as temperate spring days arrive, many Hispanic villages such as Llano Quemado attend to the task at hand: remudding or plastering adobe structures before the summer rains arrive. By slowly building up layers of mud plaster, these *enjaradoras* will secure the *pretil* (firewall) of this building. The *pretil* in a flat-roofed building is usually the architectural feature hardest hit by the weather; it usually gets a thicker coat of plaster.

Horno Building

Anita Rodriquez and Carmen Velarde, both from the Taos area, are New Mexico's most famous *enjaradoras.* They are also licensed contractors whose adobe fireplaces are highly prized. Their earthen creations are considered works of art.

Both of these Hispanic women have been honored for their work and are often commissioned to travel out of their home state as consultants to architects and builders of fine adobe homes. Both have done much to continue the centuries-old tradition of women working with adobe, and they have inspired a new generation rediscovering adobe as the path to self-reliance. Not only are they master *enjaradoras,* they both are master *adoberas,* capable of working in every aspect of adobe construction.

This level of accomplishment requires many supplementary skills, such as the techniques of *alisando. Alisando* requires the ability to produce fine earthen plasters, with a working knowledge of types of clays, micaceous materials, and proper mixtures and curing times. This knowledge can be as complex as that of the Pueblo Indians' best potters.

In New Mexican Hispanic villages and Indian pueblos, the skill of *horno* building is considered an artistic talent. The *horno,* or outdoor adobe oven, was introduced by the Spanish settlers to New Mexico and the Pueblo Indian villages. Like the so-called kiva fireplace, this development served both peoples well.

At the Museum of International Folk Art in Santa Fe, Anita Rodriguez demonstrates *horno* construction. She shapes a standard adobe into a wedge shape with a small hatchet. The shape is critical in making the adobes fit tightly in a circle. (An adobe form may also be created especially for this purpose.) Broken pieces left over from shaping the standard adobe are placed in the middle to form the interior base. The base and foundation of the *horno* must be strong enough to support the heavy adobes used in its construction and also to withstand the intense heat the oven will produce.

As the adobes build up, each row is laid to taper inward to shape a dome. Wet, dark mud is swirled over the adobes, forming a crude coat of plaster. At this point, the *boca* (mouth) is shaped. The *adobera* (woman adobe mason) now begins to determine the height of the *horno*.

El humero (the flue) has been created to vent wood smoke away from the fire. A rough plaster coat is used to shape the smoke hole. Before the rest of the mud plasters are applied, the entire structure must be wetted with a spray of water for better adhesion. Because a single thick coat of mud may crack, a number of thinner coats are recommended.

After the shaping is complete, the final plastering of the *horno* starts in earnest. First, the mud must be thoroughly mixed with straw. To make the mud flow with the lines created by the adobes, many *enjaradoras* prefer to use their hands. This gives the *horno* a sculptural, hand-coiled design. For the base, it is best to use a trowel to create a hard, sloping edge to guide rainwater away from the *horno* and give it a finished appearance.

Once the plastering is completed, the *horno* must be checked for even drying. Slow drying is preferred; a fast set might cause cracking from severe contractions. As drying begins, the dark brown color begins to mellow to a natural buckskin shade. In some areas, red or yellow pigments in the earth produce *hornos* of soft pastel colors.

Hornos at the Martinez Hacienda appear dwarfed by a
cottonwood tree stretching toward the sun. Early tourists to
New Mexico mistook the *horno* for a doghouse!

Hornos like these, in a typical Hispanic village setting, have baked bread for countless travelers and merchants coming up the Camino Real from Chihuahua, Mexico, into Santa Fe during the colonial period. The long wooden paddle resting on the single *horno* is used to pull steamy, fragrant, fresh bread from the *horno*'s interior.

Mistakenly called a *descanso* by art and architectural historians, this building in reality is an *oratorio* and may be the last of this architectural type standing in New Mexico. This *oratorio* at the Penas Negras cemetery, near Taos, was recently restored under the direction of Corina A. Santistevan. She describes the *oratorio* as a place where women would pray the rosary around the coffin while the men dug the grave of a departed villager. The structure undoubtedly deserves historical recognition because of its uniqueness and its strong architectural character. The frieze may date from the middle 1800s; the structure itself may be older.

The name of the cemetery, Penas Negras (black rocks), derives from the black lava used for headstones. Some are incised with a cross.

The interior mud plaster of this *oratorio* is almost
luminescent, adding to the sense of the mystical. Countless
visitors will pay homage here to the memory of their
ancestors in the *Camposanto.* This meditative space is a
reminder of the times when priests were few and far between,
and religious practice was left up to the Hispanic villagers
themselves. The *nicho,* where the crucifix rests, was probably
carved out of the adobe to hold it.

The wooden trim over the entrance to an *oratorio* at Piedras Negras is a recent replacement of the original design most likely created by Leandro Martinez. His home, which he built in 1862, employs an identical design on the *portal* (porch).

Mistakenly called the third order of St. Francis by nineteenth-century writers, Penitentes are a lay brotherhood of devout Christian men who dedicate their lives to imitating Christ and Saint Francis of Assisi through personal example and ritual. During Holy Week, especially during Good Friday services, some brotherhoods reenact the Santo Encuentro, in which one group carries a likeness of Mary and another group carries one of Christ. During this procession, the painful encounter of Mary meeting Christ for the last time in his mortal life is recalled with emotion and reverence. Though many nineteenth-century writers criticized the Penitentes' practice of flagellation, few appreciated the important role they played in the community as preservers of faith and community service.

Moradas (Penitentes' chapels) are usually found in tranquil settings. Some, far away from towns and cities, have been victims of marauders in search of prized Penitente folk art. This *morada*, like many throughout northern New Mexico, is dutifully cared for by the brotherhood. The *morada* preserves the religious history of its community and is as sacred to Hispanic life as the kiva is to Pueblo Indian society. Soon a multitude of hands will communally place a coat of natural mud plaster on the building, a traditional ritual.

Before replastering the *morada* in natural mud, the earth itself must be screened to remove sticks, stones, and other debris that will catch the trowel and blemish the plaster. Once the soil has undergone a number of screenings, it is ready for application.

Even if the mud mixture is perfect, the *enjarador* must gauge how thick each application must be and determine how much force must be applied for the plaster to adhere to the wall. Here, ancient coursed adobes seem almost new, protected by frequent remuddings.

With trowel and hawk in hand, the *enjarador* will start from the top of the wall and slowly work his way down to the base of the wall. In communal projects such as this, a number of *enjaradores* will work at the same time. Trowel marks left behind by the plasterers will be eventually smoothed out, free of obstructions or rises. The smoother the plaster, the less chance that rain or snow will affect the surface.

Details

EVEN THE MOST HUMBLE historic adobe structures contain a myriad of details that add grace and style and reveal the owner's aesthetic values. Details in many adobe buildings leave a historical record of the occupant's skills, whimsy, and daily preoccupations.

Though the 1930s may be remembered for bootleg whiskey and the Great Depression, it also brought the WPA projects in art and oral history. That era also produced the Historic American Buildings Survey, which captured in drawings minute architectural details, such as a rawhide latch on a door at Acoma Pueblo. Another drawing reveals a disused corn chute covered with glass at this same pueblo. In some cases the drawings, such as the carved beams in these plans, reveal the influence of Spanish friars. No detail was too small for the survey: it noted carved doors and the puncheon door, also known in New Mexico as a *zambullo* door. Because both Indian and Hispano suffered a shortage of iron for hinges, locks, and latches, they both employed a door that hung on pintles, peglike extensions of one of the vertical framing stiles. As Bainbridge Bunting noted, "because the pintles fit into sockets sunk in the sill and the lintel, such a door had to be hung before the lintel was fixed in place and could not be removed without demolishing the wall."

Details such as these are significant in light of the fact that the *zambullo* door has been traced back more than five thousand years, to the Near East. It spread to northern Europe, then Africa via Arab traders, into Spain, and then to the Americas.

The simple *nicho* (niche) in a Hispanic or Indian home was specifically created to hold a *santo* (saint). The more *nichos* there were in a home, the more saints the occupants prayed to. It is said that when a patron saint failed to grant the owner's request, the saint was turned to face the wall in its *nicho* until the prayers were answered. Today a *nicho* may hold pottery or sculpture that has no connection to its original religious purpose.

Details not only reveal necessity, skills, whimsy, and aesthetics, but also materials and styles in vogue. It is not unusual to find an adobe home with different types of ceilings; older adobes often possess the stamped tin ceilings that came into vogue in the early 1900s. Many restorers prefer to work on rooms according to historical period details, while others prefer to go back to only one period or style, Spanish-Pueblo revival or Territorial, for example.

All historical period details known in the Southwest as Pueblo, Spanish, Mexican, and Anglo have contributed to the uniqueness of adobe structures, and adobe has accommodated all of them with grace.

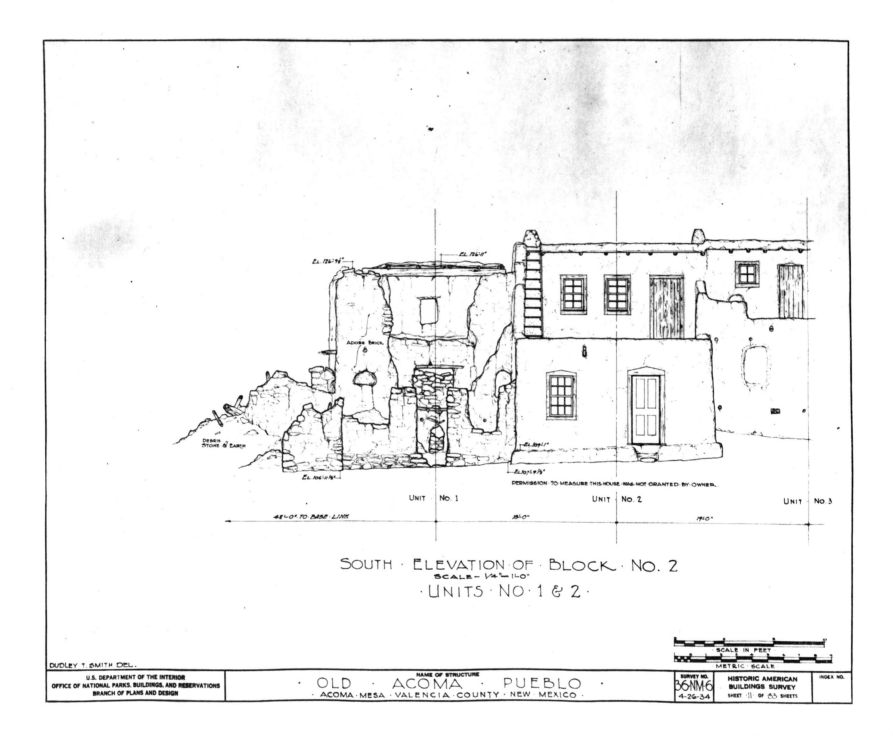

EL. 126'-9⅝"   EL. 126'-11"

ADOBE BRICK

DEBRIS
STONE & EARTH

EL. 109'-1"

EL. 106'-11⅛"   EL. 107'-9½"

PERMISSION TO MEASURE THIS HOUSE WAS NOT GRANTED BY OWNER.

UNIT   No. 1   UNIT No. 2   UNIT   No. 3

48'-0" TO BASE LINE   18'-0"   19'-0"

SOUTH · ELEVATION · OF · BLOCK · NO. 2
SCALE-¼"=1'-0"
· UNITS · NO 1 & 2 ·

SCALE IN FEET
METRIC SCALE

DUDLEY T. SMITH DEL.

U.S. DEPARTMENT OF THE INTERIOR
OFFICE OF NATIONAL PARKS, BUILDINGS, AND RESERVATIONS
BRANCH OF PLANS AND DESIGN

NAME OF STRUCTURE
· OLD · ACOMA · PUEBLO ·
· ACOMA · MESA · VALENCIA · COUNTY · NEW · MEXICO ·

SURVEY NO.
36·NM·6
4-26-34

HISTORIC AMERICAN
BUILDINGS SURVEY
SHEET ·11· OF 83 SHEETS

INDEX NO.

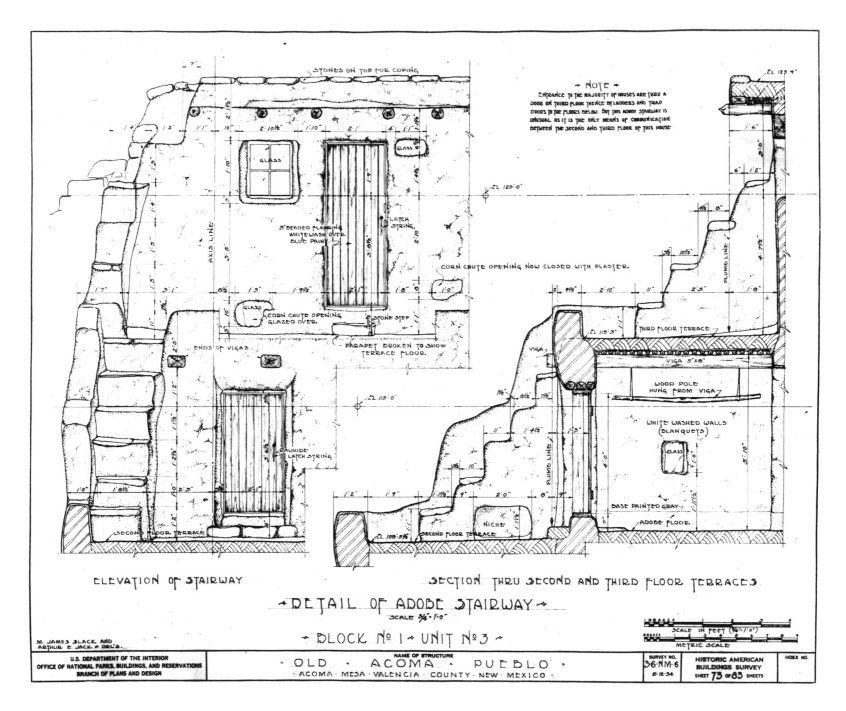

ELEVATION OF STAIRWAY   SECTION THRU SECOND AND THIRD FLOOR TERRACES

~ DETAIL OF ADOBE STAIRWAY ~

SCALE ¾" = 1'-0"

~ BLOCK Nº 1 ~ UNIT Nº 3 ~

M. JAMES SLACK AND
ARTHUR E. JACK ~ DEL'S.

U.S. DEPARTMENT OF THE INTERIOR
OFFICE OF NATIONAL PARKS, BUILDINGS, AND RESERVATIONS
BRANCH OF PLANS AND DESIGN

NAME OF STRUCTURE
· OLD · ACOMA · PUEBLO ·
· ACOMA · MESA · VALENCIA · COUNTY · NEW · MEXICO ·

SURVEY NO.
36·NM·6
8·12·34

HISTORIC AMERICAN
BUILDINGS SURVEY
SHEET 73 OF 83 SHEETS

INDEX NO.

The Historic American Buildings Survey was directed at creating "a permanent graphic record of the existing architectural remains of early dwellers in this country." Today the visual and schematic record has captured the details of Acoma Pueblo and shows how the Spanish influence was built on to a remote community that had been living high on the mesa for many generations. Note the defensively placed corn chutes and the rawhide latch strings.

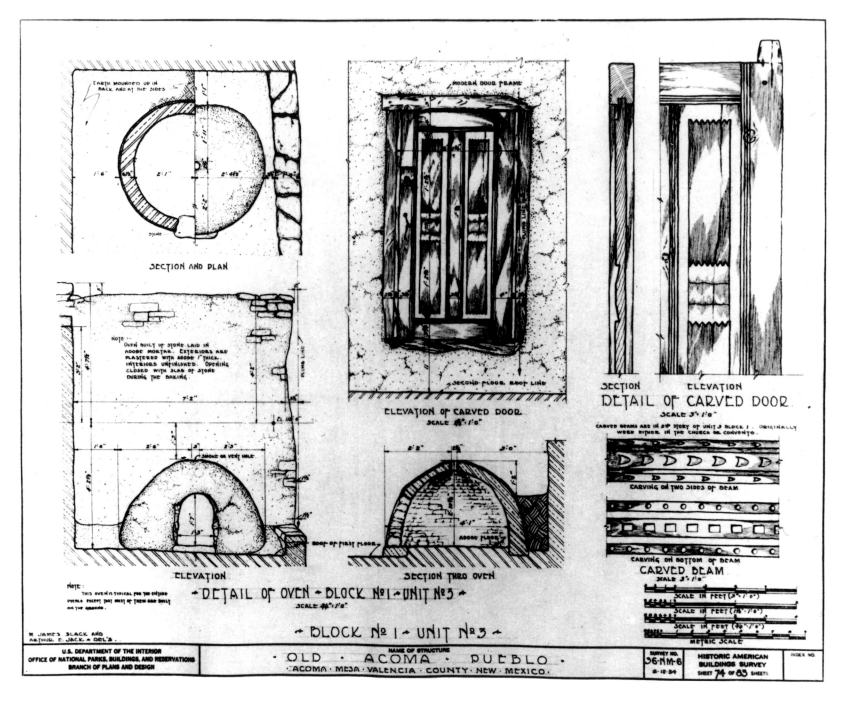

It is unlikely that the careful drawing and recording of this pueblo would be allowed today. Acoma's tribal council forbids photography within the mission buildings and allows only supervised tours to certain sections of the village.

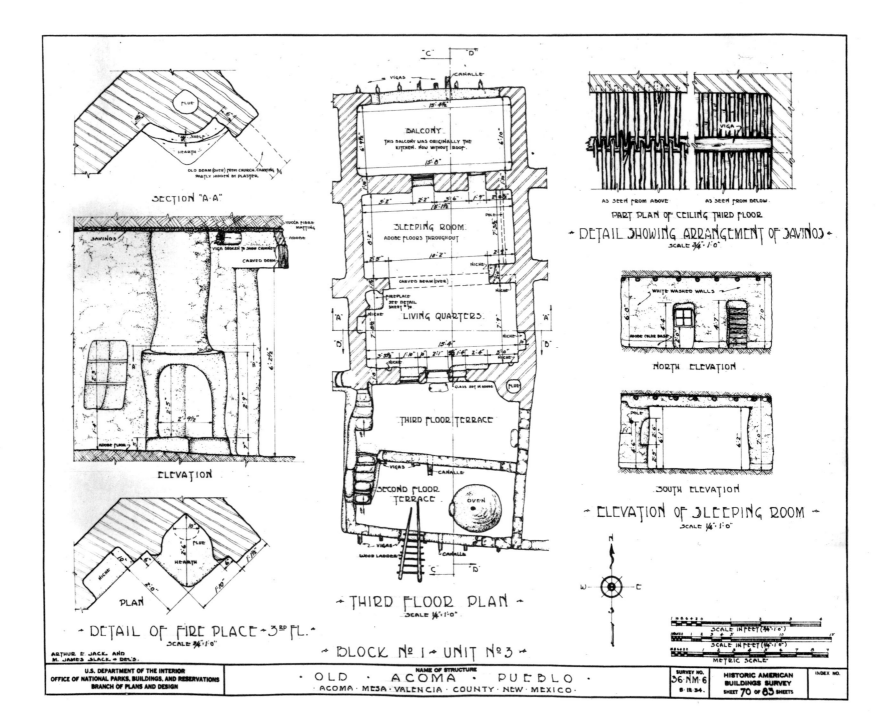

SECTION "A·A"

ELEVATION

PLAN

· DETAIL OF FIRE PLACE · 3ᴿᴰ FL. ·
SCALE ¾" · 1·0"

ARTHUR E. JACK AND
M. JAMES SLACK · DEL'S.

THIRD FLOOR PLAN
SCALE ¼" · 1·0"

· BLOCK Nᵒ 1 · UNIT Nᵒ 3 ·

PART PLAN OF CEILING THIRD FLOOR
· DETAIL SHOWING ARRANGEMENT OF SAVINOS ·
SCALE ¾" · 1·0"

AS SEEN FROM ABOVE.   AS SEEN FROM BELOW.

NORTH ELEVATION

SOUTH ELEVATION

· ELEVATION OF SLEEPING ROOM ·
SCALE ¼" · 1·0"

METRIC SCALE

U.S. DEPARTMENT OF THE INTERIOR
OFFICE OF NATIONAL PARKS, BUILDINGS, AND RESERVATIONS
BRANCH OF PLANS AND DESIGN

NAME OF STRUCTURE
· OLD · ACOMA · PUEBLO ·
· ACOMA · MESA · VALENCIA · COUNTY · NEW · MEXICO ·

SURVEY NO.
36·NM·6
8·12·34.

HISTORIC AMERICAN
BUILDINGS SURVEY
SHEET 70 OF 83 SHEETS

INDEX NO.

The Spanish settlers who arrived in New Mexico in the late 1500s and early 1600s brought woodworking tools more efficient than those of the Pueblo peoples. Much larger rooms were the architectural result. The Spanish preferred a uniform room width of about fifteen feet, with varying lengths. The wider rooms were made possible by extending the span of the walls and ceilings through longer, larger vigas that, before the appearance of Spanish tools, were more difficult to cut and transport to the building site.

Vigas, the round ceiling beams usually of fir or spruce, are a must in building a classical Spanish-Pueblo Revival adobe home. The spaces between the vigas are traditionally covered with *latillas* of materials such as split cedar (called *rajas*), aspen, willows, or narrow tamarisk to form the ceilings. *Latillas* may be laid diagonally or in herringbone patterns.

A family of means could have vigas hand adzed to form square beams. These beams, with carved corbels at each end, would usually grace a long, spacious room called a *sala* (parlor). *Salas* traditionally were used for festive occasions such as weddings, dances, baptismal parties, greeting dignitaries, or an occasional fandango.

Upon the arrival of the Anglo American, many vigas were covered with *manta de techo* (cheap muslin cloth). This type of ceiling made it possible to catch dust and other debris that floated down through *latilla* ceilings. The muslin was wetted with a mixture of flour and water, and then stretched across the vigas to form a kind of ceiling plaster. These ceilings were the forerunners of gypsum board or drywall ceilings and the more pleasing coved plaster ceilings.

Although fairly contemporary, the coved-plaster-and-round-viga combination adds a touch of elegance to an adobe home.

71

Everyday architectural elements in the Southwest were often enhanced with elaborate carvings, an artistic legacy from Franciscan friars who taught Indian laborers. From the mission churches to the most humble adobe homes, carved corbels, lintels, doors, and wooden trim enhanced the adobe immensely.

This weathered full corbel, post, and lintel combination is particularly significant: the corbel and lintel supporting the roof are of one piece. A great deal of careful planning went into the construction of this porch, probably because the heavy weight of an adobe firewall above the protruding vigas required support.

Where the porch comes out of an adjoining wall, a half corbel protrudes to support the lintel. The lintel has been notched to accept the vigas of the porch.

An array of chip-carved corbels and square beams illustrates the quality of fine detail in classic adobe construction. Corbels may be found not only in Spanish and Mexican adobe architecture but also throughout the Islamic world. Carved corbels and beams evoke a time when decorative design in adobe building was as vital as the structure itself. A ceiling like this fills the viewer with wonder.

right
A half corbel and lintel offer minimalist chip carving but much-needed support for a protruding square beam. Most round or square beams left beyond the adobe wall are done so intentionally in a style called Spanish-Pueblo Revival. All protruding beams or vigas should be capped with some form of flashing in order to prevent wood rot from entering the interior section of the beam. Barely visible, this flashing will give this beam a long life.

Looking more like an adobe walled entrance to an Islamic city in the Middle East, this highly stylized adobe wall is actually in Santa Fe. The fired tiles capping the wall continue the curl motif sculpted into the design above the entrance; they also act as protection from persistent rain or snow. Red fired tiles are of recent import to New Mexico from Mexico, but are quite common in California and Arizona where they were fired locally.

These Territorial-style gates get their name from the period
in which New Mexico was a territory, 1850–1912. The advent
of this type of gate, with its cut-out designs and add-on
moldings, resulted from an abundant supply of sawn lumber,
a variety of woodworking tools, and an attempt to mix Greek
Revival style with local folk art traditions. Anglo-American
styles, coming mostly from the East via the Santa Fe Trail
and later the railroad, were to strongly influence Hispanic
carpenters up to World War I. The 1930s and 1940s witnessed
a concerted effort to return to Spanish Colonial designs.

right

Entry gates open up to a profusion of bloom resembling a
suspended fireworks display. The native, drought-resistant
chamiso plant is a natural for southwestern gardeners and
landscapers because of its profusion of yellow color in the fall
and its low maintenance.

The hand-adzed frame and doors below re-create a style that developed when sawn lumber was scarce. Gates of this style were usually large, made in pairs, and very sturdy in order to allow animals, wagons, and supplies quick passage in the event of Indian attacks, which besieged Pueblo Indians and Spaniards alike.

These shuttered windows appear to be set too low, yet exterior elevations in old adobe structures may differ radically from interior elevations. It is not unusual to find a drop of three feet or more when entering an older adobe building.

The small, curved entrance is the restorer's way of dealing with this tiny space. Originally, this house was an adobe abode for chickens. As a reminder of the structure's humble beginnings, the chicken run was left, and the small gate retained.

right

Lack of window glass during the seventeenth and eighteenth centuries made large windows in New Mexico almost nonexistent. Because mica and selenite could be mined only in small sheets without breaking, the size of the available sheets determined the size of the window. Not until Indian raids on both Hispanic villages and Native American pueblos subsided were large window openings widely employed, and most of these were either heavily shuttered or grated. Selenite and mica windows could be found as late as 1881 at Zuni Pueblo.

Unlike pitched roofs whose water may be diverted by gutters, the flat adobe structure's minimalist drain is handled by *canales*. In this case, treatment involved sculpting a hard surface plaster to form part of the *canal*; it appears to be part of the wall.

Canales are important to a flat adobe building—without them, an entire adobe wall may erode and collapse because of a leaking water spout. These *canales* are made of hollowed logs lined either by metal flashing or rain gutters cut to fit the logs. *Canales* must be well maintained; they are most susceptible to damage and leakage at the point where the roof meets the *pretil* (inside firewall). Hard plaster can hide moisture seeping in from a leaking *canal*, which eventually weakens the adobe wall.

The decorative, handcut grates below this *canal* (water spout) vent a roof area; they are reminiscent of Spanish Colonial style.

Protruding vigas and carved adobe walls are essential
elements of Spanish-Pueblo Revival style. It combines
building styles of the Spanish and Pueblo Indian peoples,
who have lived side by side for four hundred years.

The Resulting Shape

ADOBE is to the mason what clay is to the sculptor. After complying with formal construction principles, the adobe builder enters the realm of the sculptor. Adobe lends itself to a multitude of forms. At times adobe buildings challenge logic in their massiveness and whimsical exaggerations.

One wonders if many of these adobe creations aren't the result of once inhibited children, now as adults releasing their creative inclinations in mud. But the resulting shapes are not merely childlike. They evoke a complex spiritual and intellectual heritage. Because adobe is so complex but plastic and innocent, it is easy to confuse its results with the mud cakes we made as children. Because wet adobe mud and straw stir ancient memories when one is working it, past histories in building are evoked. Just laying the adobes connects the mason to Mesopotamia, the great pyramids of Mexico, seventeenth-century Salem, and the Indian and Spanish Southwest.

The hard, cold facts are that adobe is an unsophisticated building material that demands strong arms and a stronger sense of purpose and determination. This low-tech stuff results in primal yet glorious forms of architecture that not only defy straight lines but also convention.

Adobe is also the poor man's sculpture, which provides both shelter and beauty from mud that is flared, peaked, carved, and shaped into something as simple as a buttress or a curved windowsill. Try doing that with fired brick or two-by-fours. It is no wonder that the senses, even of the novice, are fired up, enthralled, mystified when we experience the beauty of adobe for the first time. It is as if we have been awakened to a past truth when our ancestors made shelter out of the first thing they touched—the earth itself.

Described by many as the most photographed church in America, the San Francisco Mission Church at Ranchos de Taos was built in 1815—an immense, almost heroic act of discipline and creativity. Most of the mission churches took years to complete because of their extraordinary proportions. The church is built in a cruciform pattern; the buttresses appear to be sculpted mounds born of the same earth that makes up the adobe walls of the church. The structure is a magnificent example of adobe's aesthetic appeal, poetic strength, and enduring viability.

Shadows from massive protruding beams stripe the textured adobe-style stucco, adding to the exotic quality of this very American building.

High-rising buttresses, delicately carved and sculpted almost to a point, serve the double purpose of keeping walls from leaning outward and shedding moisture, which they do more readily than a wider buttress.

The Pueblo

Taos Pueblo is witness to the durability of adobe. Already centuries old when Spaniards arrived in the New World in the 1500s, most of the pueblo's walls were constructed using the puddling method. The work must have been painstakingly slow, as each wet course of mud had to dry to some degree before the next course could be applied. Ladders, a feature of most pueblos, are reminders of an earlier period when they were a defensive necessity. When enemies attacked, the ladders were raised to prevent access. Ground-floor doors were added when these attacks subsided, after the Spanish military presence afforded the pueblos more protection.

The term used by the Spanish colonists to describe town or village is *pueblo,* and since the 1500s the term has been used to describe the groups of Native Americans the Spaniards found settled along the Rio Grande.

Much like the villages of Spain, the Pueblo communities clustered around central plazas (squares) with easy access to kivas and other religious ceremonial grounds. The Spanish that settled among or near the Pueblo villages created their own form of *pueblitos* (small villages) with mission churches dominating their central plazas.

During the sixties and seventies, HUD tried to force wood-frame construction on the Pueblo Indians, who had for centuries constructed their houses out of puddled earth, then with adobe bricks introduced by the Spanish. A number of Pueblos resisted this foreign method of construction, but eventually all new federally funded housing projects in these ancient villages were not adobe but frame structures made to look like adobe.

In Taos, as in many pre-Spanish-contact pueblos, people lived communally in multistoried buildings, with different families occupying different rooms and only a narrow adobe wall between living spaces. Remudding and plastering of these natural adobe structures every two years or so, depending on the weather, is done communally.

After the reconquest of 1693, many Pueblo people returned
to their homes. As architectural historian Bainbridge Bunting
has noted, "As each group was subjugated, its members were
required to return to their old home, or, if too few in number,
to consolidate with another group. Reoccupied pueblos like
Acoma, Zia and Isleta were rebuilt using old foundations . . ."
The Pueblo V style of architecture dates from this time.
Reconstruction of Acoma continues to this day, for its
preservation is required for ceremonial purposes.

Another feature of Pueblo V period construction is the corner fireplace, introduced by the Spanish. These adobe chimneys indicate the proliferation of mud-brick fireplaces.

Acoma Pueblo, perched atop a 375-foot, 17-acre sandstone mesa, is a wonder to behold. Its mission church, San Estevan, has been called the noblest in the Southwest.

Yet Acoma is a testimony to the ironies of history. It was destroyed by Juan de Onate in reprisal for the death of his nephew and indigenous resistance; a kindly Spanish priest helped inspire the Acomans to reconstruct their pueblo and its church.

Nothing today describes this citadel in the plains and its rebirth better than Fray Francisco Atanasio Dominguez in 1776:

> This mesa has some crags around it, some of which rise to a third of its height and others halfway up, and there are some corrals for livestock on them, to which they climb by little paths which the Indians have made. In other places there are such horrible precipices that it is not possible to look over them for fear of the steep drop.
> Although I have not spent so much time at the beginning of my description of other missions as I have here it is because there is no comparison with the situation here. The little I have said to begin with at those places indicates in brief to the judicious reader the nature of the buildings and transportation in relation to the nearby rivers and easy transportation of all necessities. The contrary is true here, for there is not even a brook, earth to make adobes, or a good cart road. Therefore it is necessary to prevent any preconception in order to achieve even a confused notion of this place. This makes what the Indians have built here of adobes with perfection, strength, and grandeur, at the expense of their own backs, worthy of admiration.

Although ladders are a familiar architectural feature of many Native American pueblos, their use has become limited. Before 1700, fear of attacks from Ute, Apache, Comanche, and Navajo tribes made the ladders necessary. Once the fear of attack began to subside, there was less need to live on upper levels of community houses. Thus, more single-story buildings were erected, incorporating doors and windows. And as Bunting has noted, "Such a change was only sensible considering that heretofore fuel, food, and water for household needs had been carried up several levels on rickety ladders by the women and children."

The north wing of the Palace of the Governors sits under the crownlike tower of a nearby structure. This section of the palace exhibits vintage presses. Under the auspices of Pamela Smith, master printer, this humble adobe has seen the production of a number of fine hand-printed, hand-bound limited editions. The Palace of the Governors itself is the oldest continuously occupied public building in America today. The fact that it is adobe and possibly dates to 1610 should convince us of adobe's desirability and durability.

The Spanish used the word *estufa* to describe the underground rooms they encountered in the late 1500s. The term implies *stove*, as they believed kivas possibly to be sweat baths. It is possible they also believed kivas were meant as protection against severe New Mexican winters. Gaspar de Castano described Pecos Pueblo in 1591 in the following manner:

> Most noteworthy were sixteen kivas—all underground, thoroughly whitewashed, and very large—constructed for protection against the cold, which in this country is very great. They do not light fires inside but bring from the outside numerous live coals banked with ashes in so neat a manner that I am at a loss to describe it. The door through which they enter is a tight hatchway large enough for only one person at a time. They go down by means of a ladder set through the hatchway for that purpose.

When the Spanish later realized the kivas' religious function, they would become a bone of contention for the proselytizing missionaries. Many were ordered to be destroyed. After the great Pueblo Revolt of 1680, when many of the missions and Spanish settlements were destroyed, the returning Spaniards became more tolerant of the kivas.

Fray Francisco Atanasio Dominguez in 1777 described the kiva in Nambe: ". . . the chapter, or council, rooms and the Indians meet in them, sometimes to discuss matters of their government for the coming year, their planting, arrangements for work to be done, or to elect community officials, or to rehearse their dances, or sometimes for other things."

Ironically, both the kiva and the Penitente *morada* were to become suspect under the American occupation of New Mexico in 1847.

The *torreón* was the Spanish settlers' version of the watchtower. The added upper story, like the watchtowers of Mesa Verde, afforded a better view of the plains or the valley below. In most cases the *torreón* was incorporated into an outer wall in a plaza. Most *torreones* dissolved to dust when their use was no longer in demand.

La Casa de Estudillo was the main residence of the Estudillo family, a prominent San Diego family who came from Spain and lived in the house until the 1880s. It was built around 1827–1830, and by the 1890s was considered a ruin. It was reconstructed under the auspices of architect Hazel Waterman. Once you enter the *zaguan* (covered entrance), the historic structure opens up to a walled *plazuela* (courtyard). Here, coursed adobe brick walls are whitewashed in a lime plaster mix and topped with California's classic red tiles. California has a long and splendid history of adobe architecture, and both private and governmental organizations are involved in adobe preservation.

Worship

This beautiful adobe church, a reproduction of the 1711
structure at San Ildefonso Pueblo, cost an estimated 75,000
dollars and 80,000 adobes, and it took ten years to build,
from 1958 to 1968. In the true communal fashion of Indian
pueblos and Hispanic villages, every family was assessed
several days' labor and a determined number of adobes for
the construction of their church.

Cristo Rey Church is a classic example of contemporary adobe construction based on Spanish Colonial mission church architecture. Designed by John Gaw Meem, actual construction did not begin until June 28, 1939, when the first adobe was laid.

To make the more than 180,000 adobes that it took to construct the church, the field adjoining the church was plowed, and a huge mound of earth was created. It took three months just to make the adobes, and more than one hundred men to build the church, carve the corbels, and raise the massive vigas that span the church's ceilings of split cedar. The bulk of the work was done by the local native Hispano populace, which to this day feels a strong affection for their church.

previous page

Split cedar *latillas* known as *rajas* provide a textural contrast to the smooth round vigas that span the ceiling of this adobe church at Cristo Rey. When they were first placed between the vigas, the adobe church was filled with the aromatic scent of cedar.

right

The Santa Cruz de la Canada Church at Santa Cruz, New Mexico, is one of the most magnificent examples of massive adobe wall construction in New Mexico. It is also internationally known for its collection of Spanish Colonial religious art. The small south chapel is one of the two transept chapels in this cruciform church.

111

Nothing personifies the missionary zeal in the Southwest more than the adobe church. At ancient Acoma, early missionaries built a monument to a religious way of life that first came to Native Americans as an intrusion, then later was to be accepted and incorporated into their own ancient and traditional rituals. Built after 1629 and before 1641, the building in this vintage photo shows the coursed stone and adobe that makes up the walls before they were restored with recent plasters.

Massive adobe walls are what early adobe architecture is all about. This style of arched entrance can be found anywhere in the Middle East, yet it exists also in Taos, New Mexico, at the Martinez Hacienda. Simple yet exotic arched entryways like these were common in Spanish Colonial architecture when the builder decided against the use of a wooden lintel.

During the Spanish Colonial period and into the Mexican period, large haciendas like this one owned by famed Father Martinez of Taos continued to be made with massive courtyard doors. The purpose was to allow farm animals and large *carretas* (carts), like the one pictured here, easy access into the safety of the interior courtyard. Though life with the nearby Pueblo Indians had been peaceful, both groups suffered attack by nomadic tribes.

La dispensa in a typical Spanish Colonial home functioned as a pantry or cold room where meats, fruits, and vegetables were stored. Meats were hung from the ceiling on parallel wooden bars suspended by ropes. The long adobe bin to the left was filled with vegetables layered with straw to preserve them for the long winter.

Typical of Spanish and Mexican period homes, *la cocina* (the kitchen) was large, roomy, and a central point for much activity. Food was tied to the cultural traditions of celebrating baptisms, weddings, wakes, and religious feast days. This large kitchen at the Martinez Hacienda features a shepherd's fireplace that doubled as a bed. Its large hearth accommodated large cooking utensils.

A much simpler and more primitive dining arrangement can be seen in this adobe room. A small, cool room like this was an ideal retreat from the intense New Mexican sun or the heat of a summer kitchen.

Another version of the shepherd's fireplace is found in this room typical of the Spanish Colonial period in New Mexico. Sparse in furniture, it possibly shows the influence of the Moorish occupation of Spain, when sitting on cushions or rugs on the floor was common.

The large corner fireplace in this New Mexican kitchen is the focal point of the room. Known in New Mexico as a *fogón de campana* because of its bell shape, its large and double-sided hearth allowed for cooking with large pots. The house, built during the Mexican period, circa 1825, is in the Kit Carson Museum in Taos, New Mexico.

Although this interior adobe room could be mistaken for a rural settlement in the Holy Land, it can be found in southern California. Adobe's natural undulating and curving lines share a common bond throughout the world—a restrained elegance.

Adobe homes in this region were made by hand, as were blankets, furniture, chests, and candles. Though commercial wall paints were unheard of during the Spanish Colonial period, various hues of natural plasters were carefully prepared. A favorite hue was *tierra blanca* (white earth), which gave walls a soft eggshell hue.

This simple *banco* (adobe bench), created as part of the wall, answered the need for furniture to sit on. If the width of the wall allowed it, an *alacena* (built-in cabinet) was commonly built in adobe homes. Most had cabinet doors rather than open shelves.

Shelves built into thick adobe walls add sculptural quality to utilitarian purpose. Wooden boxes used to measure grain sit on these shelves. Candles were a cherished commodity on the Spanish Colonial frontier because they had to be made by hand.

This adobe granary in the Martinez Hacienda is typical of granaries found in New Mexico as late as the 1950s. The local people, including Hispanos and Native Americans, grew wheat, corn, barley, and other grains. Much of this produce became major trade commodities as well as everyday sustenance for the local people. The wooden boxes are standard units of measure used in grain trading.

130

Another version of an adobe shepherd's fireplace dominates this room on the Camino Real, the Royal Highway. For hundreds of years, merchants and settlers stopped at this hacienda in La Cienega, one of the last stops before arriving in Santa Fe. One can only imagine the relief a traveler must have felt when arriving at this *paraje* (stopping place) after an arduous journey from Chihuahua or another part of Mexico. The suspended child's cradle adds to the serenity and welcoming quality of this rancho.

An adobe room in La Casa de Estudillo in San Diego, despite some period furniture of the middle 1850s, shares the same adobe feeling found in much earlier adobes. Hand-plastered adobe walls, a kneeler, a rosary, and a crucifix add to the sense of spirituality that sustained early Spanish families who settled on the frontier.

Patrones (prominent families) throughout the Spanish Southwest led a more privileged life than the *peones*. But they had one thing in common that neither class nor wealth made different: both lived in homes made of humble adobe.

This sun-bathed adobe room in San Diego features an unusual floor treatment rarely found in New Mexico. Though some New Mexican homes did use flagstone, most floors were made of wet earth mixed with ox blood, dried and troweled to a hard finish. The advent of sawmills and brick kilns in the 1850s made wooden and brick floors popular; they replaced the mud floors that required constant attention.

This Spanish Colonial wall in New Mexico features an *alacena*
(built-in cabinet) with exposed raw adobe. When glass
became more available, *alacenas* were often converted to
windows to allow more exterior light in. Many of these
windows retained their primitive shutters.

One can only imagine the thousands of travelers, settlers, and merchants who arrived at this *paraje* along the Camino Real. Massive timbers, worn by countless travelers, seem crude next to the smoothly plastered adobe walls.

Tumacacori National Monument, forty-eight miles south of Tucson, is at a site visited by explorer Fray Eusebio Francisco Kino in 1691, where he established a *visita* (mission outpost).

Visitas were extremely important during the Spanish Colonial period. Both Spanish and Indian people depended on them for their spiritual needs. They also acted as reminders of the new religious order the friars struggled to maintain. The massive adobe missions also gave these outposts a semblance of Euro-American permanence.

When Fray Narciso Gutierres arrived in the late 1700s at
Tumacacori, his intent was to establish and build a mission
church as grandiose as San Xavier del Bac in Tucson. His
dream never materialized, but the nine-foot-thick adobe
walls supporting a three-story bell tower were no mean feat.
The complex once contained church and religious offices
with dwellings for the friars, an enclosed courtyard, and
numerous other structures.

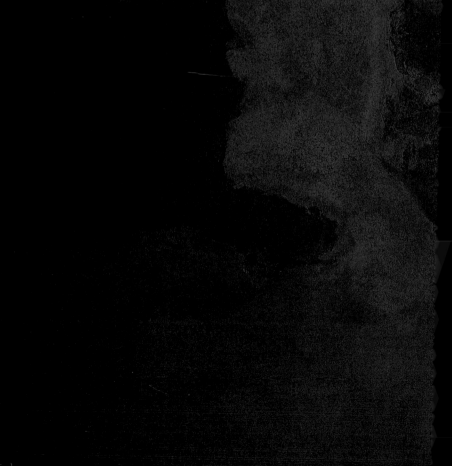

These arched doorways leading from interior spaces to
courtyards, *placitas,* or gardens are quite common wherever
adobe was used by the Spaniards. Moorish concepts of spaces
for gardens, patios, or *plazuelas* suited the arid Southwest,
which was in many ways similar to parts of Spain. An
elaborate irrigation system once watered gardens, orchards,
and vineyards here at Tumacacori. The present garden is a re-
creation of similar gardens found during the 1700s in mission
complexes of northern Sonora, Mexico.

Pitched Roofs and Logs

An often overlooked part of that architectural diversity, log buildings in New Mexico, especially in high, wet, mountainous regions, were quite common. Many were chinked or plastered with mud. Most were intended as outbuildings for storage of tools or farm equipment, or animal pens; some were used as cabins.

Outbuildings such as these were quite common in heavily forested mountainous regions. Hispanic villages such as Truchas, Trampas, Ojo Sarco, Vadito, and a host of others on both the eastern and western slopes of the Sangre de Cristo Mountains relied on log buildings for a number of uses. Many log barns had high, pitched roofs where hay could be stored for animals during the winter, also adding a measure of insulation for the animals below.

It is also theorized that many Spanish settlers used *jacales* (log cabins) as temporary living quarters until more permanent adobe buildings could be erected.

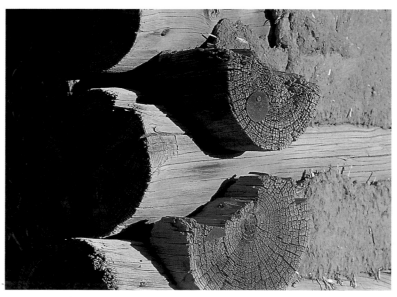

Some notching patterns in log construction in New Mexico are not found in other parts of the country where log construction was common.

Adobe played an integral part even in the construction of log buildings. This stone fireplace retains its structural integrity because of the mud used as mortar or plaster to keep the stones in place. Note the uneven ends of log walls casting shadows randomly throughout the building.

This tranquil setting in the village of La Cienega exhibits a number of structures of both adobe and logs with the classic pitched-roof styles found in mountainous regions of New Mexico. In these high-altitude areas, snow and rain are constant threats to unprotected adobe walls.

Although controversy still rages in the city of Santa Fe concerning whether an adobe structure with a pitched roof is a "valid Santa Fe style," many historic adobe buildings in downtown Santa Fe have pitched roofs. In nearby Hispanic villages, almost 90 percent of adobe structures have pitched roofs.

And it is not surprising, since most flat roofs on adobe houses have to be reroofed every six to ten years, a costly undertaking. Leaky flat roofs on adobe homes cause major structural damage to load-bearing walls, plasters, and interior spaces. The arrival of sawmills and milled lumber in New Mexico in the 1850s caused the local populace, tired of leaky mud roofs, to take to the new roofs enthusiastically, especially in the mountain villages.

The flat-roofed adobe *morada*, a Penitente place of worship and ritual on the nearby hillside, will demand more maintenance than the large adobe structure in the foreground. Time was a precious commodity at farms like this one during the Spanish and Mexican periods. Thus, the pitched roofs that easily shed snow and rain away from adobe walls eventually replaced most flat roofs.

The first pitched roofs were a board-and-batten affair, with thin boards of an inch or less laid with the slope, placed as close to each other as possible, with a second layer staggered to cover the joints. Where adobe homes were close to the railroad, the availability of metal corrugated roofing and terneplate quickly outmoded the flat mud roofs.

Much prejudice still exists against the pitched-roof adobe home. It doesn't conform to the Spanish-Pueblo Revival style that demands a flat roof and dominates the Santa Fe skyline. Yet in California, with its long history of adobe architecture and many magnificent historic adobes, flat roofs are more the exception than the rule.

It must be remembered that the creators of Santa Fe style took architectural elements from both the Spanish Colonial period in New Mexico and the nearby Pueblo Indians in the 1900s to define an architectural mode. Many architectural historians today argue that the desire to impose this romantic hybrid destroyed many valid architectural types that once gave Santa Fe a greater variety of building designs.

Although primitive by today's standards, this type of roofing not only preserved adobe walls but also, over the long narrow porches, created an attractive reprieve from the hot New Mexican sun. The *portales* (long narrow porches) were to become an integral feature of pitched-roof adobe homes.

Adobe buttresses were commonly used to keep adobe walls
from leaning out, especially when a structure was built close
to a slope. Buttresses also aided stabilization of retrofitted
pitched-roofed houses, which lacked a continuous bond
beam. High winds buffeting these retrofitted roofs could
crack adobe walls at corners or over door or window lintels.
The buttresses helped stabilize these walls.

150

This stunning example of an adobe mill with water wheel is reminiscent of the many mills established in northern New Mexico by French and Anglo trappers and mountaineers who arrived in the 1800s.

For example, Ceran St. Vrain, of French parentage, in 1864 "obtained a contract to provide flour to feed the 6,000 Navajos being held prisoners at Bosque Redondo Reservation near Fort Sumner. In 1863 he moved to Mora and the following year, built a fireproof stone mill, after his mill at Taos had been burned."

High in the Abiquiu Valley, facing toward Georgia O'Keeffe's house, is the Dar al-Islam Mosque. Designed by an Egyptian architect but built with local adobe, it is a wonderful example of the blending of Old and New World traditions.

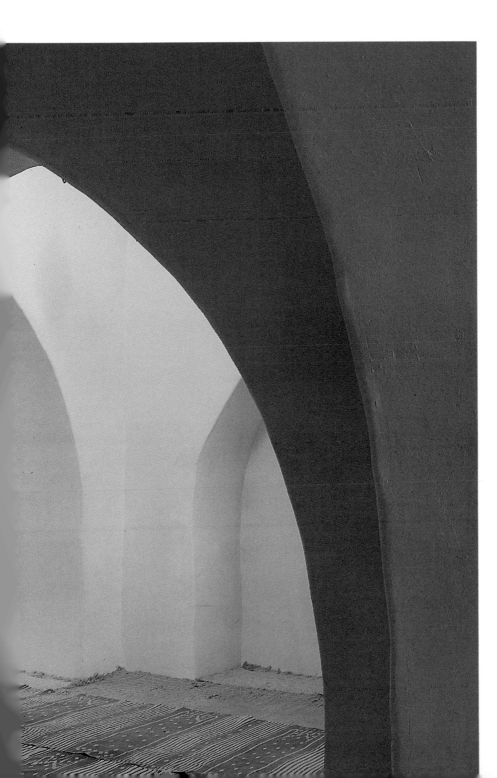

This room at La Purisima Mission in southern California was restored in the 1930s by young Civilian Conservation Corps workers who made the adobes on the site.

Artists and Adobe

"I wanted to make it *my* house, but I'll tell you the dirt resists you. It is very hard to make the earth your own."

Georgia O'Keeffe wrote these words on the restoration and building of her adobe studio-home in Abiquiu, New Mexico. As she completed her now famous adobe home in 1948, she was following in the footsteps of other artists attracted to New Mexico in the early 1900s. Few could resist sinking their hands into adobe. They had painted the adobe missions, pueblos, and Hispanic villages, and even when painting portraits, adobe walls set the background for their work. Amidst the texture and the golden straw dreams that were part of adobe plasters, these artists became engulfed in an exotic adobe world.

Where in the East could you find a Taos Indian wrapped in a blanket and leaning against an adobe wall?

Where else in the United States could you paint a portrait of an adobe *enjarador,* or plasterer, besmirched with adobe mud yet a proud and dignified sculptor in mud?

It must have been heady for these "Anglo" artists to find themselves in a rich cultural island where the native people, both Indian and Hispano, seemed to come from the adobe womb itself. In the early 1900s, almost all buildings in Taos and Santa Fe were *real* adobe, rather than veneer. Before O'Keeffe, Santa Fe's now famous "Cinco Pintores," the original five artists who founded a colony, became smitten to the point of constructing their own adobe homes along the Camino del Monte Sol.

But it wasn't just the artists, writers, poets, and bon vivants of the Southwest, such as Mabel Dodge, Mary Austin, Aldous Huxley, and D. H. Lawrence, who discovered the American Southwest and adobe's magnetism. Halfway around the world, in Australia to be exact, an artistic and intellectual colony had in its own right discovered adobe.

In the community of Eltham, a small village situated on the northeastern fringes of Melbourne, a group of creative people including artists, writers, and architects created a world of their own in adobe. According to accounts on the community, "the Eltham people resisted middle-class development. They fought for their primeval bushscapes, clay roads, indigenous trees and the natural beauty that surrounded them."

Led by the architect Alistar Knox, they changed the stereotypic thinking that relegated adobe to mud huts; they elevated it to a desirable mode of housing. In fact, "it was Eltham which changed conservative Australians from regarding all earth buildings as mud huts and gradually coming to think of them as elegant adobe residences."

But it must not have been easy for Knox. For those first creative pioneers, "it was at the time impossible to raise a loan on a mud-brick building. They tended to be an expression of an individual rather than an alternative lifestyle." It is ironic that adobe houses, both in Santa Fe and Eltham, are now considered almost exclusively the domain of the wealthy. Knox, commenting on adobe's value in Eltham, so precisely mirrors adobe's current status that one could believe he was speaking of Santa Fe today:

> There is growing evidence that mud brick properties are among the most acceptable securities on which to lend. This arises from the increasing demand by more and more people to own them and to live in them. Now they are in danger of becoming the prerogative of the rich. A significant problem that confronts earth building in today's social climate is the fact that they are fashionable and a status symbol rather than the background for creative living.

In Santa Fe, if the Cinco Pintores could come back to visit, they would probably be surprised that their five adobe "little huts" built by the five "little nuts," as they were called, would command prices of up to half a million dollars each.

The Victor Hansen residence in Santa Fe was once home to well-known Santa Fe artist B. J. O. Nordfeldt. Nordfeldt was born in Sweden in 1898, settled in Chicago, and after World War I was brought to Santa Fe by his friend William P. Henderson, who was also to become a famous artist. He spent the next twenty years primarily in New Mexico. Nordfeldt was to keep company with Gustave Bauman, Maurice Sterne, Carl Sandberg, Robert Frost, Vachel Lindsay, and a host of other artists and writers who visited New Mexico.

Detailed carving on lintels over wide adobe walls hints of an era that romanced Santa Fe and adobe architecture as an integral part of the artist's milieu. Nordfeldt's friend William P. Henderson was so taken by adobe that "he restored old Sena Plaza on Palace Avenue and designed and built the Museum of Navajo Ceremonial Art, the Fremont Ellis house on Canyon Road, and the Santa Fe Railroad ticket office on the Plaza."

Randall Davey, another member of the famed Santa Fe artists' colony, arrived in 1919. As Edna Robertson has noted, "One of the most important events to happen to the growing art colony occurred in 1919, when John Sloan, one of the great painters and etchers of the twentieth century in America, decided with Randall Davey . . . to investigate the situation in Santa Fe."

They did more than investigate; they stayed to paint and build adobe houses. The Davey house is an excellent example of a renovated sawmill and flour mill.

The Randall Davey home, now part of the Audubon Society's headquarters, is a fine example of adobe elegance and the lifestyle the successful artist courted.

The large beam in the middle of the room allows for a large area by expanding the span of the vigas that meet at the beam.

previous page

Randall Davey's studio looks much as it did during his forty-year tenure. Part of that stay included his involvement in the restoration, renovation, and addition to the buildings he bought. Davey had trained in architecture at Cornell; the adobe compound he produced was not only a release of creative energy but also a result of his trained architectural eye.

Davey's boudoir and dressing salon is an example of the artist's flamboyant style. Imagine the flickering flames in the adobe fireplace illuminating this room at dusk.

Writer Edna Robertson had said of Davey, "His personality was enchanting. He loved to talk about horse-racing, and looked like a gentleman jockey himself: small, full of tension, and beautifully dressed in boots and tweeds. Someone said that even when Randall was very poor he lived as though he were rich; certainly he was a man full of richness and joy."

Taos, New Mexico, became another artists' colony that would attract Mabel Dodge, D. H. Lawrence, and the six founding members of the Taos Society of Artists, formed in 1915.

Ernest L. Blumenschein was one of its founding members. The light that bathes Blumenschein's studio today is the same famed New Mexican light that both artists and painters raved about. The hint of gold that bounces off sculptural adobe is the same light Blumenschein gave to his paintings.

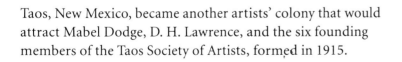

166

The intense light of this elevation is the same light that
D. H. Lawrence tried to subdue by creating these window
decorations for Mabel Dodge's bathroom. While Lawrence's
novels are bold and daring, it is said that he was a modest
man.

Lawrence's brief period in New Mexico had a profound
effect on him, inspiring him to create these simple window
decorations and to plaster an adobe *horno*. He was to
remember the area in these words:

> The moment I saw the brilliant proud morning shine high
> up over the deserts of Santa Fe, something stood still
> in my soul and I started to attend. There was a certain
> magnificence in the high-up day, a certain eagle-like
> royalty. . . . In the magnificent fierce morning of New
> Mexico one sprang awake, a new part of the soul woke up
> suddenly and the old world gave way to a new.

The cube and diamond grates, the four-paneled door with painted insets, and the decorations said to be made by D. H. Lawrence exemplify the architectural details that abound in the Mabel Dodge adobe home. Peel marks on the vigas and the curving lines of adobe walls give this hallway a handcrafted appearance.

This corner fireplace, highly decorated by D. H. Lawrence, seems more like the work of local Hispanic or Taos Pueblo artisans. The interesting feature of this adobe fireplace is the extended fire pit with a wooden frame to catch flying sparks.

Painted vigas and *latillas* at Mabel Dodge's home exemplify elements of adobe architecture that appealed to many writers and painters who settled to work in Taos and Santa Fe. This wonderful ceiling has the foreign feeling of a distant place in the Middle East.

Lush foliage frames the back entrance to a Santa Fe artist's studio. Massive adobe walls, secret *placitas*, gardens, and open patio doors like these continue to beckon artists to the Santa Fe and Taos areas. While much of the bohemian lifestyle is history, the artists' adobe legacy remains.

This corner fireplace nestles in a porch area. It allows the comfort of a fire to a person savoring the crispness of the late fall air. Many of the artists were great entertainers, and social life revolved around their adobe homes.

This humble corner fireplace is graced with priceless *santos*. *Santos* are religious images carved in the round or painted on wooden slabs called *retablos*. Devout Spanish colonists and Mexican-period citizens commissioned local artisans to create religious images for their homes. Original pieces are now highly prized collectibles. Fortunately, a new and thriving school of *santeros* continues this rich Hispanic tradition.

The stacked drums represent various Indian pueblos of the region and are a tribute to the art of drum makers, who still flourish in New Mexico's Rio Grande Valley.

Handmade Indian baskets contrast with the "American" period chest and table in this adobe room. New furniture styles were brought to New Mexico over the Santa Fe Trail. These styles were considered exotic in contrast to the homespun quality of the locals' work.

This beautifully carved lintel over a thick-walled adobe entrance expresses the creativity that adobe allows in architectural detail.

Many of Santa Fe's early artists' studios consisted of only a few adobe rooms. Far from elegant, they were practical and affordable. Up through the 1960s and 1970s, Santa Fe's moderate rents attracted writers and painters living on a slim budget. An adobe space like this one rented for about sixty dollars a month in 1969. It is now beyond the means of many painters and writers.

178

The airy living space here is the result of building around two patios. This magnificent adobe residence began quite humbly as a one-room house in 1844; by 1868 it had increased to five rooms. Documents indicate that Juan Rodriguez de Ortiz left to Maria Juana Quintana both the aforementioned house and the nearby flour mill, named *el molino de las animas,* "the flour mill of the spirits."

Adobe architecture adapts to many styles of interior design. Elegant historical objects and furnishings from various cultures and periods make each adobe home unique. The crystal chandelier amid the vigas adds a touch of elegance to this historical adobe.

In San Diego, La Casa de Estudillo, the home of a prominent
Spanish family, portrays another level of elegance,
particularly for the middle 1800s.

Perhaps the most elegant adobe structures are those with
minimal decoration and furnishings. Adobe itself is elegant,
as shown in this section of noted architect Theodore
Waddell's residence.

The Adobe Home

This idyllic setting in lush Nambe Valley was an ideal location for Spanish settlers. Although the Pueblo Revolt of 1680 drove the settlers back to El Paso del Norte, by the 1700s the Spanish and the Pueblo Indians were forming alliances to protect themselves from the attacks of nomadic tribes. Many of the adobe homes in this valley, as well as the nearby Indian pueblos, were built through the joint efforts of Hispanic and Pueblo *compadres* working side by side.

While adobe fills the senses, its creators brought to it their own spirituality. This doorway leads into a meditative atmosphere where crosses and *retablos* express the strong faith that sustained early Spanish colonists.

The beauty of natural, raw adobe plasters cannot be imitated. Golden straw particles catch the light. During wet weather, adobe in its natural state requires a significant amount of upkeep; yet many owners wouldn't have it any other way.

This six-paneled double door typifies the increasing use of milled lumber in New Mexico in the 1850s. But the raw adobe plasters are not typical. Because of the labor involved in seasonal remuddings, many owners choose the hard cement-based plasters; yet nothing surpasses the look and feel of real earth plasters.

Patio areas like these in adobe homes were constructed with a purpose. Spanish builders rarely put a window on the north side of the home but created their patios in an L- or U-shape, facing south to catch the last sunlight on fall days.

This glass-enclosed patio entrance, built before the popularity of solar homes, is evidence of early architectural ventures in using high desert light. Plants and vines thrive, dominating the ceiling. Because of adobe's thermal mass and its use as a heat sink, it is an excellent material for solar construction. Note the colonial period–style door with its raised sill.

Stories are told about the lady who arrived from New York: "I just can't possibly stay in that room. It has mud walls and these dreadful sticks in the ceiling!" When she realized that all the rooms in the inn were made of mud and all the ceilings had sticks, then she agreed to stay. "It does have some form of primitive charm, I must say." Before long she came back again and again, and finally died in a room made of mud with sticks in the ceilings.

Hand-stamped tin candleholders, gourd scoops, an old horn, a polishing stone, and wooden boxes evoke the humble adobe dwellings of the early Spanish settlers.

Adding a band of colored earth was a popular method of adorning adobe walls. Colored earths ranged from white, gessolike washes to soft pastel pinks, blues, and greens. The magnificent chest is made of milled lumber and dates from a later period than the building; it complements the small handmade doors quite nicely.

In adobe construction, corners are not sharp, rigid, vertical barriers but tapered, gently flowing lines. A weathered door, rough plank *trastero* (a pine cupboard), and brick floors give this room a sense of local history.

In adobe architecture, not all fireplaces were built in the corner, especially during the American period of occupation into the Territorial period, 1846–1911. Anglo Americans arriving from the East soon brought their own influence to adobe. It is not unusual to find different period fireplaces in an adobe house, reflecting the tastes of various owners.

In adobe homes, floors are as varied as the individuals who design them. Brick floors have become as traditional as wood planks, flagstone, or tile floors. Designs in brick express the owner's individuality.

Comparisons with Africa and New Mexico. This starkly
modern-looking exterior stairway in Mali, West Africa,
predates the picture opposite.

This hand-sculpted *padercita* (little wall), with its gentle shadows, is an entryway into the magic that is adobe.

This magnificent adobe house is an excellent example of a traditional adobe updated by allowing more exterior light to come in. Many modern adobe builders use skylights in the same way that friars in the Colonial period used clerestory openings to bathe their altars with natural light.

An *alacena* (cupboard) built into this adobe wall looks more like a New England pie safe than an early New Mexican period piece. The use of tin for decoration in New Mexico began after 1846. Tin containers for lard or lamp oil, discarded on the Santa Fe Trail, were quickly picked up by local New Mexican tinworkers to be hand-stamped and made into candleholders, cupboard panels, mirror holders, and a host of other decorative items.

Looking more like a scene from Middle America than from the adobe homeland, this potbellied stove and handmade pitchfork remind us that adobe has been used from the East Coast of our country to the sandy beaches of California.

This rough, sawn-lumber window frame with shutters was obviously installed after 1850 when the first sawmills were built in New Mexico. The saw marks complement the adobe plaster trails left by the *enjaradores*.

Natural lighting shows that these interior adobe walls are the same color as the exterior mud plasters. The exotic foreign furniture, the cut-out paneled door, and the wide-planked floor evoke a meditative atmosphere.

212

Although not built out of adobe, the home of Bill and Sunny Empie is included here because many adobe elements are incorporated into the structure. The setting itself could be called a southwestern Stonehenge—early Hohokam Indians used the boulders as shelter. When Hispanic homes were built over early Pueblo sites, care was taken to divert stem walls and foundations from structures or objects used in the past. The Spanish people called the earlier residents *la gente de antes* (the people from before), and they were not to be disturbed.

Architect Charles F. Johnson of Santa Fe designed the Empie
home with a great deal of sensitivity to the site and the
Hohokam who had once inhabited the area.

The stunning clarity of desert light and the organic
arrangement of cactuses and other natural vegetation give the
visitor a sense of stumbling into a forgotten region where
living with nature informs architecture.

A huge sculpted fireplace dominates this space. Yet the granite boulders and vigas balance it. Light meanders through glass-covered crevices in the natural stone. The hand-carved table adds to the eclectic tension created in this space.

When the Empies and the architect discovered the remains of a Hohokam period fire pit and three pots, they retained the ancient pit but constructed a new one to the right in order not to disturb the original one. As in ancient times, the chimney is built into a natural crevice between stones.

Rounded forms dominate this home, harmonizing the
gigantic boulders with smaller-scale, homey architectural
features. Boulders unite the interior and exterior, separated
only by thermal glazing.

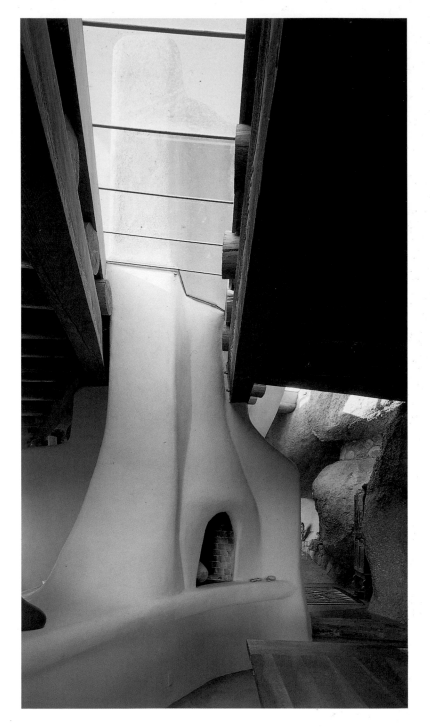

Another view of the fireplace shows the reflection of natural light from skylights above, almost bleaching its contours.

right

The massive granite boulders are kept from overwhelming the residence by the gentle adobe-style, contoured walls.

In the kitchen, light falls on sculptural shapes that complement the boulders. The stove and oven have adobe-style niches of their own.

226

Vigas radiate in almost kivalike symmetry. Ancient
architectural elements of the Southwest have been borrowed
successfully by architects and designers since they stumbled
upon this magical land of stone, mud, earth, sun, and ancient
spirits in the early 1900s.

Solar Adobe

ADOBE OFFERS THE PROMISE of minimizing the use of forest products and chemically produced building materials—its use seems as natural as the sun's rising and setting. This concept is not new—it represents the collective wisdom of ten thousand years of human use of earthen architecture. I am reminded of something I read about World War II, when "both the Allies and the Axis Powers sought to conserve energy and material resources by using sun baked earth for various types of construction. Architects as varied and well known as Le Corbusier in France . . . and Frank Lloyd Wright in America all helped to promote construction in earth between 1940 and 1945."

To many young people, World War II is not even a distant memory. Even baby boomers have only a hint of what that crisis brought home to America. GIs came home from the war to build homes of adobe in the Southwest in the tradition of their Indian and Hispanic ancestors. Many of those traditions were revived by the baby boomers of Anglo, Hispanic, and Indian parentage who in the 1960s and 1970s strove for greater self-sufficiency.

Adobe is not the historical property of one culture or people. The earth has been used for building in Massachusetts, New York, Nebraska, and other American states. And throughout Europe, adobe buildings still stand not so much as witness to the past but as reminders of what we can do to guarantee our survival in the future. And our future is based on working with the earth, not against it.

Solar Adobe

Adobe construction and passive solar energy are a marriage made in heaven. Nothing matches adobe in beauty and in practicality—its thermal mass works well in combination with glazing facing the sun.

Not that passive solar heating is anything new. For thousands of years, people the world over have oriented their shelters to maximize the amount of sunlight received during the winter months. "The world's first community planned for using the sun was probably Olynthus, built in the fifth century B.C. All houses faced south, guaranteeing access to sunlight for rich and poor alike," according to Michael Shepard. "The Greeks were not alone. Similar developments took place in China about the same time. The Romans used the sun to heat their famous baths, warmed their homes with solar heated greenhouses, and codified the first law stipulating the right to sunlight."

In the Americas, the ancient Anasazi Indians built structures facing the sun, and the Mesoamerican city of Teotihuacán was laid out on a grid facing south. The early Spanish also built their homes without north-side windows or doors and oriented their structures to the south, with courtyards and patios intended to make the most of the winter sun.

Santa Fe and northern New Mexico, maybe because of their long periods of cold but also their abundance of sunshine above seven thousand feet, have been on the cutting edge of passive solar design. Since the 1970s, the names of solar energy designers such as William Lumpkins, Peter Van Dresser, Bill Yanda, and Mark W. Chalom, to mention but a few, have captured international attention in their use of native adobe with both passive and active solar designs.

Almost all solar designers have a passionate desire to design living spaces that are self-sufficient and work in harmony with nature rather than against it. With the price of energy continuing to climb and our nation's rising fiscal deficit, a combination of solar energy and adobe holds potential for a clean break from our wasteful past and dependence on foreign oil. As master solar architect William Lumpkins has stated in his guide, which contains thirty proven plans for passive solar design, "Good luck in reducing the use of fossil fuels to the lowest consumption possible. We are running out and much faster than the best of experts will admit."

231

At first glance, this solar-designed structure appears similar to most adobe homes we've seen before. This Pueblo-style structure surrounded by native bushes requires closer examination to reveal its innovative construction. South-facing glass walls allow as much sun into the structure as possible. Energy is held in the building's interior mass.

That mass may be an insulated brick floor, a slab of dark concrete, or the adobe wall itself. This type of passive solar design is called *direct gain* because sunlight comes directly into the interior space through both vertical glass walls and clerestory openings in the roof.

The narrow porchlike overhangs above south-facing walls have been designed to provide enough shade to temper the summer sun's intensity. In addition to drapes, reflective shades may be used in the summer to avoid overheating.

Glossary

ADOBE A word of Arabic and Spanish origin, used to describe a sun-dried mud brick and the structure built from the bricks.

ADOBERO(A) A man or woman who works with adobe. Also, the term used for the wooden form in which the mud is cast.

ALACENA A cabinet built into an adobe wall.

ALBAÑIL An adobe-brick mason.

ALISANDO A plaster style requiring a specialized technique that uses a wet sheepskin to leave a smooth surface.

BANCO An adobe bench usually attached to a wall.

CANAL Water spout.

CAPILLITAS Small chapels in rural settings.

CINCO PINTORES Santa Fe's "five famous artists" and the artistic colony they established. Josef Bakos, Fremont F. Ellis, Walter E. Mruk, Willard Nash, and Will Shuster are the five artists.

COMPADRES Godfathers. At baptism, godparents become part of the extended family. In New Mexico, godparents of Hispanic children could come from the Pueblo Indian community, strengthening the bonds between Hispanic and Pueblo Indian people.

CORBEL A decorative, usually hand-carved support for a viga that projects from the wall.

COVING Water damage and erosion at the base of an adobe wall resulting from substandard footings.

DESCANSO Originally, a spot where Penitentes stopped to pray. Now used for the crosses along roads that mark where a person has died.

DISPENSA Pantry; cold storage room.

ENJARADOR(A) Man or woman who works as a plasterer.

ESTUFA The name given by the Spanish to a Pueblo kiva, meaning "stove." (A misnomer.)

FANDANGO A festive dance celebration among Hispanos.

FOGÓN Fireplace; heater.

FOGÓN DE CAMPANA Bell-shaped fireplace.

HORNO Outdoor, inverted-beehive-shaped cooking oven introduced to New Mexico by Spanish colonists.

HUMERO Fireplace or *horno* flue.

JACAL (Mex.) Upright wall made of cedar poles chinked and plastered with mud.

KIVA Usually round, subterranean, private religious structure used by Pueblo Indians.

KIVA FIREPLACE Name usually applied to the corner fireplace brought by Spanish colonists to New Mexico. (A misnomer.)

LATILLA Aspen pole or willow lath used between vigas.

MANTA DE TECHO Muslin cloth stretched over vigas or beams in imitation of a plaster ceiling.

METATE (Mex.) A curved, partially hollow stone used for grinding corn or other grains by hand.

MORADA A private religious structure used by the Penitentes of New Mexico.

NICHO Niche carved out of an adobe wall to hold the image of a patron saint.

NOGGING A building technique found in New England whereby unfired adobe bricks are laid between vertical posts.

ORATORIO A small adobe structure used for prayer. Usually a family chapel.

PADERCITA Small exterior or interior adobe wall.

PENITENTES A lay religious fraternity that assists a Hispanic community in both spiritual and secular matters.

PISÉ From the French *pisé de terre* (rammed-earth construction). Earth of various degrees of moisture content is rammed into forms directly to form a wall.

PLACITA Usually an interior courtyard or patio. Sometimes called a *plazuela*.

PORTAL Porch.

PRETIL Firewall that caps a flat-roofed adobe structure.

PUDDLED ADOBE Method of building with mud whereby layers of wet mud are directly built onto the wall and left to dry so that other courses may follow.

RAJAS Split cedar *latillas*.

RESOLANA A place, such as the south-facing wall of a home, that receives the last warm rays of fall sun. Used for social gatherings.

RETABLOS Flat slabs of wood gessoed and painted with religious images.

SALA Living room or other large room used for entertaining.

SANTEROS(AS) Hispanic men and women who continue the art of painting and carving religious images.

SANTOS Carved religious images.

TORREÓN Defensive adobe watchtower.

VIGA Round, peeled timber used as a ceiling beam.

ZAGUÁN Large, covered entrance usually leading from the exterior of an adobe building into an interior patio.

ZAMBULLO New Mexican term for a handmade door built into the door frame, whose hinge is a pintle (wooden peg).

Bibliography

Adams, Eleanor B., and Fray Angelico Chavez. *The Missions of New Mexico, 1776: A Description by Fray Francisco Atanasio Dominguez.* Albuquerque, New Mexico: University of New Mexico Press, 1956.

Bunting, Bainbridge. *Early Architecture in New Mexico.* Albuquerque, New Mexico: University of New Mexico Press, 1976.

Cruz, Gilbert R. *Let There Be Towns: Spanish Municipal Origins in the American Southwest, 1610–1810.* College Station, Texas: Texas A&M University Press, 1988.

Detheir, Jean. *Down to Earth: Adobe Architecture: An Old Idea, a New Future.* New York: Facts on File, 1983.

Dispensa, Joseph, and Louise Turner. *Will Shuster: A Santa Fe Legend.* Santa Fe, New Mexico: Museum of New Mexico Press, 1989.

Easton, Robert, and Peter Nabokov. *Native American Architecture.* New York: Oxford Press, 1989.

Fathy, Hassan. *Architecture for the Poor: An Experiment in Rural Egypt.* Chicago, Illinois: University of Chicago Press, 1973.

Fink, Augusta. *Adobes in the Sun: Portraits of a Tranquil Era.* San Francisco, California: Chronicle Books, 1972.

Getty Conservation Institute. *6th International Conference on the Conservation of Earthen Architecture. Adobe 90 Preprints.* Los Angeles, California: J. Paul Getty Book Distribution Center, Santa Monica, California, 1990.

Khalili, Nader. *Racing Alone: A Visionary Architect's Quest for Houses Made with Earth and Fire.* New York: Harper & Row, 1983.

Kimball, Fiske. *Domestic Architecture of the American Colonies and of the Early Republic.* New York: Dover Publications, Inc., 1966.

Knox, Alistair. *We Are What We Stand On: A Personal History of the Eltham Community.* North Blackburn, Australia: The Dominion Press, 1980.

Lesli, Laurie. *Portrait of an Artist: A Biography of Georgia O'Keeffe.* New York: Seaview Books, 1980.

Loomis, Sylvia Glidden. *Old Santa Fe Today.* Santa Fe, New Mexico: The School of American Research, 1966.

Lumpkins, William. *Casa del Sol: Your Guide to Passive Solar House Designs.* Santa Fe, New Mexico: Santa Fe Publishing Co., 1981.

McHenry, Paul Graham, Jr. *Adobe: Build It Yourself.* Tucson, Arizona: University of Arizona Press, 1985.

Robertson, Edna, and Sarah Nestor. *Artists of the Canyons and Caminos: Santa Fe, The Early Years.* Salt Lake City, Utah: Peregrine Smith, Inc., 1976.

Rudofsky, Bernard. *Architecture Without Architects: An Introduction to Non-Pedigreed Architecture.* Garden City, New York: The Museum of Modern Art and Doubleday, 1964.

Shepard, Michael. *Solar Remodeling in Northern New Mexico.* Santa Fe, New Mexico: New Mexico Solar Energy Association, 1981.

Smith, Edward W., and George S. Austin. *Adobe, pressed-earth, and rammed-earth industries in New Mexico.* Socorro, New Mexico: New Mexico Bureau of Mines and Mineral Resources, Bulletin #127, 1989.

Acknowledgments and Credits

We would like to thank the following for
their help in the preparation of this book:
Neyla Freeman, Tony Kramer, Sally Larkin,
Coe Newman, Neil Poese, Rebecca Romero,
Corrine Santis Estevan, Dina von Zweck.
We would also like to thank
the Governor and Council of Picuris Pueblo
for allowing us to record the rebuilding
of their church.

The photographs are by Michael Freeman
except for the following:
Eduardo Fuss 46–50; Jack Kotz 236;
David Larkin 8, 84b; The Photographic Library
at the Palace of the Governors, Museum of New
Mexico 33, 37, 44, 45, 112;
Carollee Pelos 12–15, 17; Paul Rocheleau 175, 176;
Chuck White 230, 231.

This organic architecture must welcome ancient spirits to be
at peace in this place.